HOW TO HAVE GREAT SUCCESS

HABITS OF SUCCESSFUL PEOPLE

By: Esther O. Nuel

All Rights Reserved. No part of this publication may be reproduced, distributed, or transmitted in any form by any means, including photocopying, recording, or any other electronic or mechanical methods, without the prior written permission of the publisher, except in the case of brief quotations embodied in critical reviews and certain other non commercial uses permitted by copyright law.

TABLE OF CONTENTS

INTRODUCTION

To everyone who deems it fit to walk down the road to achieving great success, it becomes a very cheap and easy task to carry out. But to him that is timid and not willing to take a bold step will end up seeing the road as too far, resulting in failure.

Literally everyone has plans at the beginning of every New Year, yet only a few achieves their aims at the end of the year. Not just a mere occurrence, but two things are involved: Willingness to pursue target and Unwillingness to pursue due to circumstances that surrounds the target.

People that fall into the category of those that do not end up meeting their set goals, they only need to make a new resolution and take few practical steps. Then, they are back on the track of achieving even greater success.

As you delve into this book, make that resolution to take the bold steps needed to kick start on the road to success. And if you need to get better in your success journey, inspire yourself the more, as you read through these factors that aids great success.

If you want to succeed, you need to work harder on your attitude, than you do on your job.

CHAPTER 1
THE ATTITUDE FACTOR

The first and major factor that enhances success is 'ATTITUDE'.

Attitude is the totality of a man's life. His behavior or character that is seen outwardly comes from the inward attitude.

One may tend to keep his attitude, to hold good records, but definitely, it reveals itself in the day to day activities of the person, because attitude cannot be kept for so long. Attitude is like a smoke that cannot be hidden.

John C Maxwell said; "Attitude is an inward feeling expressed by behavior.

This is why an attitude can be seen without a word being said."

In achieving success, attitude plays a vital role. Whatever attitude you portray towards that task plays out as the end result. It is not a magic, one who feels reluctant in keeping the home tidy, will end up sleeping in the mess, while one who gets up to do necessary things can never sleep in mess.

This above logic is applicable to all aspects of life. Success does not make you a winner; your attitude towards the success makes you a winner. Attitude makes all the difference in your life.

Clement W. Stone says; "There is little difference in people, but that little difference makes a big difference. This little difference is 'ATTITUDE'. That big difference is whether it is positive or negative.

The fact is that; life is 10% what happens to man and 90% of man's reaction. You are in control of your attitude.

POSITIVE ATTITUDE

People with positive attitude tend to make it earlier and cheaper than others.
Below are a few reasons why it is so.

- ❖ They believe they can do all things, no matter how difficult it seems.
- ❖ They are never scared of little beginnings.
- ❖ They go for what they want against all odds.

- ❖ They are always ready to pay a price called perseverance.
- ❖ They are not afraid of mistakes; rather, they learn to do better next time.
- ❖ They grow through difficulties.
- ❖ They are goal oriented, so they strive for excellence always.
- ❖ They are never ready to settle for mediocrity.
- ❖ They are always in search of something good in all situations.
- ❖ They never take negative thoughts or advice.
- ❖ They see opportunity in every difficulty.

Making positive attitude a lifestyle, definitely will birth great success.

Nothing can stop the man with the right mental attitude from achieving his goal; nothing on earth can help the man with the wrong attitude. – Thomas Jefferson.

NEGATIVE ATTITUDE

Below are some reasons why people with negative attitude find it difficult to end successfully.

- They give up too early.
- They let negativity choke them, making them doubt if what they started can end well.
- They do not believe in little beginnings, they want cheap success.
- They easily become afraid of making mistakes.

- ❖ They have the "What If" Problem. 'What if I get laughed at?'
- ❖ They are not goal oriented.
- ❖ They barely see good things in all situations.
- ❖ They see difficulty in every opportunity.

Know this; if you desire constant success, you must work on having the right attitude. Scott 37Hamilton said; the only disability in life is a 'Bad Attitude'. A bad attitude is like a flat tire; if you don't change it, you are not going anywhere.

Attitude is the key to getting everything right; it will either be your best friend or worst enemy.

CHAPTER 2
THE POWER OF VISION

After we have discussed thoroughly on the first and major factor of success which is 'Attitude', the second and important ingredient is 'The Power of Vision'.

Ability to see with the eyes of the mind is termed 'VISION'. One essential quality of those that are successful is their ability to see ahead of others, they see what others do not see.

Vision is the ability to see beyond impossibilities; seeing useful opportunity in every difficulty, in order to make meaning out of a meaningless situation.

Winston Churchill said "The empires of the future are the empires of the mind".

Vision equips you to see and pursue a desired future, it inspires your commitment, and what you see determines your destination. If you see success, you get success and if you see failure, you get failure.

Ken Guab said; "when you limit what you think you can do, you really limit what you can accomplish". Without vision you cannot be motivated, because your vision is the force driving you.

"A man without a vision is a man without a future. A man without a future will always return to his past". P. K. Bernard.

Hellen Keller said, "The most pathetic person in the world is someone who has sight but no vision".

Men of vision are men who leave legacies for posterity not just because of their length of days but because of their large dream.

If you do not have a clear vision, it's likely that you will ponder a lot and waste a lot of time and energy. Not sure what you should be doing, or what you could be doing.

You can also question whether your life even counts, as a lot of other individuals do.

The normally unremarkable parts of our life are given meaning via vision. Let's be honest. When seen in the context of a greater goal, a lot of our everyday actions don't seem to matter very much. But as soon as you connect the details of the day-to-day with a clear goal, meaning emerges! All of a sudden, there's purpose and drive!

VISIONARIES ARE ACHIEVERS

In life, everyone ends up someplace. A small number of people go someplace on purpose. Those are the ones possessing a definite dream and vision.

A successful person may have additional advantages. They do, however, have vision. Someone once stated that if you aim for nothing, you will always succeed! I completely concur. A well-defined vision can substantially enhance both your life and your business.

In the meanwhile, put the following into consideration. They can assist in igniting the process of picturing or having a vision:

- What are your goals?
- Why are you motivated to accomplish it?
- What advantages come with carrying it out?
- What are the drawbacks of not completing it?

Right now, resolve to dedicate several minutes to addressing these four questions. They may surprise you with what they disclose.

How To Have Great Success

CHAPTER 3
CONFIDENCE/COURAGE

Having a clear vision and the bravery to follow through on it can greatly improve your chances of success. It really is that easy. You are significantly more likely to feel fulfilled and significant in life when it is purposeful and well-focused.

Confidence is a feeling or that you can do something well or succeed in it. It makes one feel certain that something is true. We all need confidence to succeed in life.

Confidence is the opposite of fear, with confidence, you can conquer any giant, and you can do the impossible. Life becomes a rewarding adventure.

Having confidence sometimes makes all the difference between success and failure. With confidence, you have ended well even before starting.

If you want to achieve success, you need to have courage. It's so simple. Courage is the quality that enable us take risks, face challenges and push past our fears. Without courage, one can never step out of comfort zones or pursue dreams.

IMPORTANCE OF COURAGE

Courage is more than just being brave; it is the key to unlocking our full potential and living a fulfilled life.

Courage/ Confidence involve 4 things:

- ✓ Hopefulness in the face of misery.
- ✓ Persistence in the face of antagonism.
- ✓ Daring in the face of risk.
- ✓ Acting in the face of struggle.

Courage rules out thoughts of fear in us.

Norman Vincent Peale said; "Think courageously, act courageously, and fear will yield to courage".

Less Brown said; "Too many of us are not living our dreams because we are living our fears".

What Fear Does/Attributes of Fear:

- Fear weakens purpose and drive.
- Fear changes focus.
- Fear crushes expectations.

- Fear prevents from making important changes in life.
- Fear cripples creativity.
- Fear does not give anyone access to anything good.

The state of your mind is also important to take courageous actions. If fear is allowed in your mind, taking bold steps becomes difficult.

Dale Carnegie (1888 – 1955) American writer said; "You can conquer almost any fear if you will only make up your mind to do so. For remember fear doesn't exist anywhere except in the mind.

"If you have no confidence in self, you are twice defeated in the race of life". Marcus Garvey.

Confidence has been one of the strongest weapons of great achievers. Having fear within you will not make you achieve your goals. Be bold enough to stand and take courageous decisions that matters to you becoming successful in the journey of life and never allow or take negative thoughts within you. It will only make you fret and lose focal point.

How To Have Great Success

CHAPTER 4

YOUR ENVIRONMENT

Environmental factor is another important thing to consider in achieving success, because the environment influences people's behavior and motivation to act.

Your success in life may also be influenced by the location in which you reside. There will be more chances for networking and meeting possible clients or consumers if you dwell in a major city.

However, if you're just starting out, living in a major city may also be incredibly costly, which might strain your budget. Nevertheless, living in a smaller location might also be less costly, giving you more financial wiggle space as you walk through achieving your aims.

ENVIRONMENTAL INFLUENCE ON YOUR EMOTIONS

➤ Feelings and health.

Your environment may affect your feelings, whether you recognize it or not. Although this varies from person to person, mood is often influenced by a room's size, color, décor, orderliness, and other features.

For instance, a disorganized home might lead to extreme tension. After all, knowing that there are clothes all over the bed or dirty dishes in the sink might make it difficult to unwind completely.

> Motivation to work

Most individuals find it quite difficult to keep motivated while working from home. If you are in an environment that either not conducive or messy, you may find it difficult to focus.

> Interaction

Humans are social animals, that much is certain. In actuality, social interaction is vital to our health. Even the most reclusive individuals need companions or family. On the other hand, several researches have connected greater levels of wellbeing to increased output and superior quality of work, which is known to increase the likelihood of professional success in the future!

As you can see, you could not even be aware of the effects your environment has on you! You may change even apparently little elements, like the color of your walls or a disorganized living area, to boost your confidence and increase your chances of succeeding.

Whether you know it or not, you are influenced by your surroundings all the time—literally, around the clock. This has the potential to either be a positive force that supports you in achieving your objectives and succeeding in life, or it may destroy your hopes and aspirations.

Your surroundings include basically everything that you spend most of your time with, the people you follow on social media, the things you read, listen to, and watch, the place you work and live in, and a lot more.

The harsh reality is that everything in your environment has an impact on your ideas, assumptions, motivation, mentality, standards, and self-imposed objectives. In fact, you are only as excellent as your surroundings.

We believe that we have power over the things we say, think, and do. But in actuality, we are mostly products of our surroundings. We are, without even realizing it, typical of the world around us.

Consider your living or working space.

Consider your interpersonal connections. Consider the many sources of distraction in your life. They may be sociable; they may be a means of self-medication or diversion; do they bring out the best in you?

You need to begin removing yourself from that setting if they aren't. You need to surround yourself with people who will only see the best in you and who will encourage the changes you want to make to your behavior and mentality.

Your success is greatly influenced by your surroundings. If you haven't previously given your surroundings any thought, now is the perfect moment to do so in order to maximize concentration, productivity, and success.

It's not necessary to make all the changes at once. You may begin by compiling a list, then go over each item on the list one at a time.

CHAPTER 5
TAKING RISK

Taking risks involves doing things that might end up being unfavorable, pursuing a course of action and disregarding a chance for danger.

The inclination to indulge in actions that carry a possibility of hurt or hazard but also have a chance for a favorable result is known as risk-taking.

Acquiring sufficient information and pursuing an objective despite unfavorable conditions is risk-taking. We have to be willing to take risks if we want to succeed in life.

Iveta Cherneva said; "Only those who play win, only those who risk win.

History favors risk takers, forgets the timid, everything else is commentary".

Keeping to comfort zone does not take anybody far; the more the risk, the higher the payoff. If you don't take risks, you won't advance. Pain comes before gain, and struggle comes before prosperity.

You are never too young or too old to pursue success or your aspirations, vision, and objectives, regardless of your current age.

In this era, risk-takers are the high flyers and trailblazers. Your next risk determines how great you will be; those who are afraid of danger cannot succeed.

Lots of people "love to play it safe." This is the domain of mediocrity. It is the home of the common person. They always follow the rules and color within the lines. They seldom, if ever, go beyond the borders because they are afraid of the unknown.

Those who "play it safe" are dependable. They live a normal existence with regulations. Their decisions are often influenced by what other people think. This is the group that fights to maintain the status norm.

Risk-takers are a distinct kind. They inhabit the world of potential and grandeur. They don't hesitate to live beyond the bounds and to express themselves creatively. Failure is only defined by failed experiments, in their opinion!

Those that take risks are known for their zeal and spirit of adventure. The applause from the audience doesn't really bother them. They are more concerned with making the most of each and every second. They dare to "bravely venture where nobody has gone before" without fear.

People that challenge norm and push the boundaries of what is possible inspire us. Contrarily, mediocrity lacks inspiration. It also doesn't result in greatness. No matter how you define it, you won't achieve success unless you're prepared to go beyond the boundaries that both you and other people have set for yourself.

Every significant historical innovation in science, business, sports, health, and other domains may be traced back to a single individual who dared to take a risk rather than play it safe. People who are successful are aware of this. Their sense of adventure leads to their creativity. Because they have the courage to live above the ordinary, they create, accomplish, exceed, and prosper.

DEFINED RISK

Successful individuals do take risks, though they don't take careless chances. Only an idiot jumps in. They may behave in a way that observers see as foolish, yet that couldn't be farther from the reality.

Great leaders and doers take calculated chances. They consider all of their alternatives and ponder things thoroughly. They study and get the information required to decide wisely. They assess the benefits and drawbacks.

Obtaining important information has never been simpler in the modern age. It's easier than ever to weigh your alternatives, do your research, and "get everything you need to know".

However, what distinguishes successful individuals from others is that they take action after doing their study! They make the move. They dare to go forward. They face the threat!

ACTION IS NECESSARY FOR SUCCESS.

A lot of individuals have objectives. Seldom do they ever come true. A lot of individuals have dreams. Seldom do such aspirations come true.

People who are successful know that dreams cannot be brought from the realm of the ethereal into the physical world without taking risks. Having a vision is one thing. Being a visionary is something else entirely.

Think back on your aspirations and ambitions for a minute. Consider the risks you may need to take as you go over them in order to achieve them.

Are you prepared to take a chance on failure, misunderstanding, mockery, etc.? If so, you could achieve success and feel the excitement of exclaiming, "Wow... I did it!"

How To Have Great Success

CHAPTER 6
INFORMATION FACTOR

One characteristic that sets successful individuals apart from others is their passion for the pursuit of knowledge. People who are passionate about knowledge and utilize it well will undoubtedly succeed since they have a stronger advantage over others who lack this passion.

Lack of knowledge will cause you to overspend on important aspects of your life and to use more strength and energy.

Billy Graham said; "The theme of our generation is; get more, know more and do more. Instead of pay more: be more and serve more".

Knowledge separates the successful from the unsuccessful.

WHY INFORMATION IS LOVED AND SOUGHT BY SUCCESSFUL PEOPLE

o Your life style is determined by the amount and quality of knowledge you possess.
o Information provides you bravery or self-assurance in your line of work.
o Information elevates the level of living and gives life meaning.
o Information also enables people to achieve greatness.

o If you lack information, you will be flawed.

WAYS TO GET INFORMED

❖ Keep on learning

Learn all you can until you are a wealth of information. Since knowledge is life, the day you stop learning is the day you start to die. Life is an educational process that never ends.

Socrates said; "Employ your time in improving yourself by other men's writings, so that you can gain easily what others labored for".

❖ Continue studying.

People and future generations won't have an option but to listen to you if you dedicate yourself to lifelong learning and study, as well as appropriate application of the knowledge you acquire.

 A life of study is necessary to ensure a bright future and for those who are willing to pay the price, resources and knowledge are hidden gems available in books, periodicals, online etc.

❖ Spend time and money developing your ability.

Attend lectures, gatherings, and quiet times; peruse the memoirs and life stories of accomplished individuals. To avoid making the same mistakes they did, learn from their successes and failures.

Develop your abilities, sharpen your intellect, and increase your capacity to absorb and apply what you have learned.

❖Follow up attentively.

Listening to others benefits you more. There is sense in gibberish, therefore pay attention to both wisdom and folly. Don't be the one to speak all the time. Pay attention to knowledgeable individuals, including senior and junior colleagues.

❖Always inquire

Asking for directions will ensure that you don't get lost. Because someone else's knowledge begins where yours ends, you are not an island. To increase your ability, you should constantly be open to ask questions. You inquire from people to get facts.

How To Have Great Success

CONCLUSION

SUCCESS AT LAST

Having thoroughly discussed the success determining factors in this book, it is already an established glaring fact that your success is in your own hands.

You are solely responsible for all that you encounter on your journey to success, no one will be held accountable if you eventually take a turn back.

Your success or failure can never be determined by people, they can only be an access port or hindrances on your way.

Put into practice all that you have learnt in this book, beginning with having the right attitude towards success. You will be surprised that your attitude will help a lot.

People without a right attitude can never go far in life, they just merry-go-round the same spot.

Proceed to having a clear vision towards your goals. With the right vision, you will only see opportunities of reaching your aim even in difficulties. One with the right vision cannot be stopped.

On to the next which is confidence. Success is never gotten without courage or confidence. You need to be brave in taking difficult decisions that may even seem impossible, but with courage, you will come out successful.

"Success is not measured by what you accomplish, but by the opposition you have encountered, and the courage with which you have maintained the struggle against overwhelming odds". Orison Swett Marden

Your environment is another key factor that aid or mar your success journey. Sometimes, you need to work on your surroundings to be effective in your success journey; this may include changing the set of people you mingle with, if they are not inspiring you.

You need to be in the midst of people who encourage and desire to see you succeed at all cost.

Taking risk cannot be left out when it comes to reaching your goals. If you are scared to take risk or you always want to play it safe, then you are not ready for success.

"Success is to be measured not so much by the position that one has reached in life, but by the obstacles which he has overcome". Booker T. Washington

However, its important to take calculated risk. Successful people do not jump at something without cross examining it.

Finally, gathering enough needed information to be empowered is necessary to enhance your success journey. Only someone who loves information gets success at a very cheap rate.

Empower your mind with the right resources and success is already at your fingertip.